Customize Your Home Theatre

5.1 channel to 15.2 and everything in between

By Anthony Di Chiaro

Published by:

Voltaire Publishing Company

www.voltairepress.com

Copyright 2014 - Voltaire Publishing Company

ISBN: 978-0-9773092-6-9

Contents:

Introduction

Introduction:

Is it just me or does it seem entirely too expensive these days to go to the movies? When you do finally go to the movies are you left feeling disappointed and cheated out of your money? What if you could make your own home theatre instead?

Perhaps you have a home theatre, but would simply like to make it sound better. I will show you how you can make adjustments to your existing home theatre to do just that. Don't have a home theatre, but have heard of others having them and you just feel way over your head in how to even get started? Not a problem. I will explain it all in simple steps.

Once you are ready you can follow the rest of my instructions and vastly improve what you have way beyond a 5.2 or 7.2 channel system. How about an 8.2, 10.2, 11.2, 12.2, 14.2 or even a 15.2 channel surround sound system? Certainly this would be the envy of the neighborhood!

You see, the problem with going to the movies is this:

1)   The cost of tickets just keeps going up, while DVD's have not. In fact, Blu-Ray's are quite affordable most of the time. Streaming services are very affordable. I use several to keep my costs down.

2)   It is not convenient. First you have to find out what is playing and when, and then make preparations to drive there. Gas prices continue to be on the rise. It saves me both time and money by watching movies at home.

3)   Wanna know how to squander away money really fast? Just go to the concession stand and see for yourself! How much for a soda and popcorn or candy? Really, that much? You could have bought the movie on Blu-Ray or DVD next month when it comes out and saved a bundle!

4) Once inside you have to try to find a good seat and then even if you do get one, who's to say that someone really tall won't decide to sit directly in front of you in the next row only to block your view of the movie?

5) Be wary of low budget priced theatres too! I took the kids to one recently and I have never been so disappointed! This was supposed to be a treat taking them to a movie. There we are (myself and my three kids) sitting down to enjoy a film. The movie was playing with just a sound bar and a subwoofer. It would have sounded much better at home.

6) Let's not forget the three other common mishaps at the movies: Gum on the floor, sticky seats and my favorite; the people who won't stop talking.

7) There is no intermission at the movies. There is however, at my own home theatre. I can always press pause whenever needed for a refill, to use the bathroom or simply to get up and stretch.

Let's take the home theatre journey together!

Chapter 1: Speakers and their general placement

Placement of your speakers, you will find, can adversely affect the sound you hear. For example: placing a speaker on the floor will increase the bass, while simultaneously reducing the clarity and volume of the sound produced.

On the other extreme, placing speakers above ear level will make them play much louder and clearer, however the bass will be almost non-existent.

If you place the speakers away from a wall they will appear louder and have less bass. If you put them up against a wall some bass will return. The most bass comes from placing speakers not just up against a wall, but also directly up against the ceiling.

Since nothing prevents the sound from bouncing off the ceiling it is the bassiest of all. In home theatre you want all speakers (except the sub) at ear level if possible when you are seated.

Also, you want to aim them all at a fixed focal point. I aim them all so the middle seat of my couch is the best seat in the room.

Other factors include the type of flooring you have in the room, the room size, the shape of the room, the height of the ceiling and the furniture arrangement.

Carpet will deaden the sound. If you do have carpet, as most of us do, simply put your speakers on speaker stands (even if they are big 12's).

Try not to place a speaker within a few feet of a sofa or it will muffle the sound.

Satellite speakers and especially bookshelf speakers work well in small rooms such as bedrooms and dens. Large living rooms and perhaps great rooms and basements should have larger speakers in them to produce the sound clearly without having to crank your receiver up.

Tile flooring, if all by itself, can create an echo effect and so can vaulted ceilings. If you do have tile flooring you will want to invest in a nice big throw rug to put in the middle of the room. If you add the throw rug you will get the best of both worlds; bass that's lively and also very loud and clear sound. Carpeting the walls from baseboard level to about three maybe four feet up will help too!

Do not put your home theatre into a room with a pitched ceiling. A raised ceiling is going to create an odd, annoying echo. An L shaped room, or any room that is not enclosed on all sides will negatively affect how well sound can be heard.

Also, when I watch movies the only lamp on is a clampable desk lamp and it is bent toward the floor and is about 4 or so feet behind my couch so there is no glare. Any lamp that can create indirect lighting and aimed low will work just fine.

To counteract open spaces, try this (it's cheap and can be easily removed). Take a tension rod and put curtains on the tension rod. I use noise reducing ones that also block out most of the sunlight. Hang the tension rod up to help block out the light and to keep the sound from escaping the room. I did this in my L shaped great room and it helps. Whenever I want to watch a movie I hang this up to divide off the kitchen from my home theatre. Now even during the middle of the day I can make it dark enough to feel like a dimly lit movie theatre!

Never turn up a receiver more than half way. Doing so can strain the receiver and cause clipping to your speakers which will damage them both.

While I am discussing receivers, which do you think is better to do when on a tight budget…? Should you buy a cheap, low powered receiver and really good speakers to get you by for now? Or, should you buy a really nice powerful receiver and buy cheap speakers for now? The answer will probably surprise you.

The answer is to buy the nice powerful receiver first. You should do this so you do not damage your speakers. High-end speakers typically have both a minimum and a maximum volume level. Using an underpowered receiver will damage both the receiver and the speakers.

Chapter 2: Subwoofers

Before explaining subwoofers, I want to start off with a few questions.

Why do you think some people run dual (two) subwoofers and not just one? Granted, having two subwoofers provides you more bass, but do you really need them both?

The answer is yes, you do...if you really want the best sounding home theatre possible for where you live or you just truly hate your neighbors.

Currently I live in a 2nd floor apartment and I run a 10.2 channel surround sound system. Yes, you heard right 10.2! This system is capable of easily being expanded all the way up to a 15.2 channel system. Later on I will explain exactly how you, too, can have this setup in your home theatre. So as I was saying, I run dual subwoofers which, like all of my speakers, are strategically located for optimal sound.

Subwoofers are typically placed directly on the floor and are up against a wall. When subwoofers first came to be, they were referred to as "down firing" and "passive subwoofers." The idea was to send the lower (deeper) frequencies from smaller less capable speakers and re-route them to a much larger, more capable speaker. Later this was dramatically improved upon and has evolved into the subwoofers we use today.

Today's subwoofers ("subs" as they are now commonly referred to) are not "passive" and instead have their own amplifier ("amp") to make the sound sent to them from the main speakers or directly from the receiver much more powerful. Also, the speaker part of the cabinet they sit in is no longer "down firing" (aimed directly at the floor) and instead is now "front firing" (aimed directly at a wall). This was improved upon because sound sent from a cabinet sitting only about ½" to 1" above the ground was immediately deaden by carpet. Only if the floor was tiled did the sound actually have a chance to travel and make any impact on the sound.

Earlier I mentioned that my dual subs are strategically located and here is how:

1) My smaller sub is an 8" 50 watt powered sub turned up ¾ of the way. It is placed on a solid wood board that is twice the size of the sub itself. The board sits directly on my carpet. The speaker part of it faces a wall and sits only ½" from the baseboard. The board it sits on (because it's solid wood) helps counteract the carpet from deadening the sound. This way I feel the bass travel across the floor right up to my sofa that sits eight feet away.

2) My more powerful sub is purposely chosen as the sub to fill in the whole room with bass. This way, I do not hear the bass in one corner, which I personally feel is distracting from both music and movies. The way I have arranged this sub is how you should setup a sub if you only have one sub. I have this sub aimed ½" from not one, but two walls. That's right, I put it in a corner and angled it between the two walls. This sub, by the way, is a 10" 100 watt powered sub. By placing it this way the sound it produces appears stronger since it has more wall space to bounce off of. I then took it one step further. I placed this sub on a raised platform so it sits approximately 6" off the ground. This was done to make the sub appear even louder and clearer. This sub is turned up ½ way.

Placement of the sub matters more than how powerful the sub is. I used to have a dual 12" sub (two 12's in it) with a 600-watt amp. At one house I had it placed in a corner right up by the baseboard but sitting directly on the floor. It shook the walls and worried me that it would shatter my very large single pain glass window I had in the room, just a few feet from it. I could actually feel the glass flex some.

What was even more impressive was that the opposite wall it was on was actually being shook enough to rattle the kitchen cabinet doors that hung on the other side of the wall.

At my next house I used the same sub and it never even came close to my bass output of the sub I have today. This is because it had to sit on the carpet in a corner behind a couch. Subs need to be in the left or right corner beside the TV.

Chapter 3: "Makeshift Sub"

This allows for louder sound without damaging your pair of speakers. This makeshift sub helps provide some additional bass. To do this splice wires and take half of the sound (both left and right) that would normally go to a pair of bookshelf or satellite speakers and run it to a single larger speaker. The other half of the left and right sound connects the smaller speaker like normal. Mine was a pair of 5.25's to an 8".

Next, cover the mid and tweeter with cardboard. (The cardboard can be removed later.) Place the grill on like normal and it will, most likely, hold the cardboard between the grill and the speaker cabinet.

Then prop this speaker up a few inches from the ground and place it against a wall (or better yet, place at the corner of two walls). Basically it creates a passive sub when you do not already own a passive sub.

Your receiver will know that this is an additional speaker added to it even though it is not plugged directly to the receiver. It is important to note that if by creating your own passive sub you are using more speakers at a time than what your receiver is designed to handle, it will automatically power down the receiver for safety.

If for example you are running a 5.1 channel receiver and you want more bass from music and are playing it in a 2.0 surround sound this will not be an issue. If however, you are using the same receiver for a movie in 5.0 surround sound your receiver will power down because it is not designed for this additional speaker.

The point one (.1), just so you know is for a dedicated powered sub. If you have no powered sub hooked up to a 5.1 channel system you are using it as a 5.0 system.

Chapter 4: Main Speakers

These are the speakers that are the most important when listening to music. In a perfect world, you would have two systems in your home, one for home theatre and the other just for music. I say this because no matter how many speakers I listen to - and it's been quite a lot - I am still torn on what is the best to use.

I will never forget a neighbor I had about 10 years ago. I owned my own home at the time and I had my slider open to my back yard and heard, to this day, the loudest and clearest speakers I have ever heard! It was so loud and clear it was as if I was at a concert only better because it was an outdoor venue without any noise from the crowd. The vocals sounded absolutely perfect. The sound engulfed the neighborhood and I was unable to pinpoint its location or even its close proximity to me.

I then closed the slider and opened my front door. Upon opening the door I was instantly blown away by the deepest bass ever with zero distortion and believe me when I tell you it was loud! At this point, I was able to immediately pinpoint its exact location. It came from my neighbor's house located directly across the street from me and it was playing from inside his garage. The garage door lay open only a couple inches off the ground.

I later got to know my neighbor and discovered why this system was in the garage and not inside his home. His wife wanted a normal living room, free from massive speakers and so their living room had a Bose home theatre in it.

People always ask me what I think of Bose. I will never knock a competitor, so here is all I will say "Bose is the industry leader in surprisingly good sound out of tremendously small speakers." This is designed for small rooms and lots of people are happy with this. What I have found, in general, is that small speakers can fill a room and Bose is the best at this, until you play music. Obviously, my neighbor agreed with this or he would have gotten rid of this setup of his.

As it turns out, he was running a pair of 18" 3-way ported speakers in hard wood cabinets, driven simply by a 100 watt per channel receiver with both adjustable bass and treble. He had a graphic equalizer to further optimize the sound, but it was not even connected to anything. Also, he had no subwoofer, just a CD player.

In my findings, I do not like to use small speakers for music. Some have come a long way and sound amazing. Right up until I play the same music with larger 3-way speakers, that is. You see most bookshelf speakers are 2-way and not 3-way speakers. The difference is a 3-way has a dedicated midrange. Without the midrange, vocal clarity is not the same and literally not there to be heard. Satellite speakers have no midrange so how can they accurately play your music? The answer is, they can't.

Currently I have a pair of 5 ¼" 2-way ported bookshelf speakers that are down-right amazing in a medium sized home theatre setup. They are better than some 3-way speakers I have heard even when playing music. However, my no name 3-way 12's make music so much better. I simply turn on the dual subs and lookout below and beside me (literally)!

With movies, however, most 2-way bookshelves are just fine. Try to make the tone match for the center channel. Because I enjoy movies and music both so much, I had to go with 12" 3-way speakers in my living room. Once I made that decision, having mid size speakers with them just didn't sound right. This is because the main speakers end up out-playing the surround sound speakers even if your receiver lets you adjust each speaker's volume independently. This is why my setup that I am using involves large speakers everywhere. Also, I found that my music was lacking when using 2-way speakers.

Update:

Recently I stumbled across an old-school pair of name brand 10's. They are ported in the front and are only 2-way. I paired them with an old-school name brand pre-amp and connected a DVD player (for use as a CD player) and a MP3 player to it. They both had to be connected with RCA cables.

I found out that I could be (and was) wrong about music with 2-way speakers. Apparently with a good stereo driving really good speakers music really can be great, even with 2-way speakers! However, remember this is the exception to the rule about using 3-way speakers and not the rule! Now I use one system for music and another for movies.

Chapter 5: Surround sound speakers

These are referred to as "surround speakers" and "surrounds." When most people talk of these, they typically are referring to the rear left and rear right speakers found in a 4.0, 5.0, 5.1 and 5.2 channel setup. Others talk about these also as side left and side right speakers when talking about a 7.1 or 7.2 channel setup.

"Surround sound speakers don't matter that much." I have heard this all too often over the past couple of decades and I am here to tell you they are both right and wrong. Allow me to elaborate on this one. Here is what I say to this... If you follow everyone's advice and use small or just plain basic speakers then, yes, they are right in saying that they do not matter much. If however, you use good 3-way speakers, you will discover just how wrong they are.

Case in point, back in the days of VCR's I watched the movie *Star Trek First Contac*" with my 5.1 channel setup that I had back then. This is a great movie by the way! My surrounds were 8" 3-way bookshelf speakers and it sounded good. I played it again just minutes after swapping out those 8's for another pair of 8" 3-way bookshelf speakers. The first pair went down to 80hz; the second pair went down to 65hz. The difference was night and day. It wasn't just that I was watching the entire movie over again and simply did not notice something in the background the first time. No, it was as if the surrounds had their own soundtrack playing, a soundtrack that simply was not there before!

So, ponder this... if that much music and effects were gone using medium to large size speakers that were the same size as the first pair and simply had a better frequency response, then just how much am I missing when using cheap small 2-way speakers? What is actually playing out of those crappy speakers anyway? Not much. And with those hooked up, you will come to the same conclusion everyone else has been saying for decades:

"Surround sound speakers don't matter much."

In conclusion if you don't care much about surround sound, then save money and buy cheap speakers. If however, you're like me, buy the best you can at the time and upgrade gradually as you can afford to. If you don't want to feel like you're in the middle of the action when watching a movie, then why are you bothering to purchase a surround sound system or even this book?

Chapter 6: Center Channel

When building a home theatre, the single most important speaker is not the pair of front speakers as most people think. The center channel (sometimes referred to as the "center") steers not only the center of the action in a movie, but also the dialogue. In fact 70 to 80 percent of all sound in a movie is set to come out of the center channel. A good center channel speaker can play from 80 HZ (70 HZ if you're lucky) to 20 KHZ.

Have you ever tried to watch a movie with a weak center? I have, but only until I could get something better. Typically small centers cannot be turned up enough to be heard clearly especially when trying to decipher the dialogue being said in a movie.

Small centers are typically cheap to buy because they use small tweeters and woofers. These small speakers are unable to recreate the clarity necessary, nor are they powerful enough to handle additional volume. Since we immediately turn up the volume in a futile attempt to hear what we missed, let this be a lesson to you, don't buy a cheap center! In this case "you really get - or don't get - what you did or did not pay for."

I have experimented over the years with many different centers. My first was a cheap single 3 ½" woofer with no tweeter at all. Boy was that crap! You see, you need the mid range speaker which would be the woofer in a center channel speaker cabinet for mid range sound (your sub will handle the bass). The tweeter is for the high sounds such as an opera singer hitting the high note or the breaking of glass.

Next I had a nice center with dual 5 ¼" woofers and a ¾" liquid cooled tweeter. It was a BIC and it also had a rear bass port, built in circuit protection and banana plug connectors. Most speakers have liquid cooled tweeters now. This is because at high volumes paper cone tweeters get too hot and die. This is commonly referred to as being "fried."

In retrospect I should have kept this one. Instead, I "upgraded," or so I thought. My "upgrade" was to a ridiculously large center designed to fit across the entire length of my 53" rear projection high definition television that I had at the time. This center speaker had four 5.25" woofers, a rear bass port and a 1" liquid cooled tweeter. The speaker was marketed very well as being the ultimate center. It was twice the size of the BIC I had, and it sat right on top of my TV. It actually weighed 30 pounds! In truth, it was crystal clear and was capable of endless volume. However, the BIC, if turned up some could play just fine.

My next center was, like all of them, a name brand. This one had the best bass tone to match my super bassy 12" BIC's that I had at the time. It did however, have one drawback, it was too bassy with its rear bass port and dual 6 1/2'" woofers and a 1" liquid cooled tweeter. No matter how much you turned it up it was just too bassy to clearly hear the dialogue spoken.

Currently I use much weaker no name 12's and an old 8" 3 way bookshelf speaker without a bass port as my center. My center can handle a good amount of power, and I can actually hear the dialogue like I should. What an amazing concept! Best of all the tone is similar sounding to the 12's I am currently using so it sounds like it belongs there.

Another good use for this is to connect it to a basic receiver for another room. Take an audio out cable (2.5 MM or 3.5 MM depending on your computer) and plug one end into your computer's sound card. Plug the other end into your receiver. For this to work one of the cables needs to be an RCA cable. No splicing is needed since such a cable already exists. Plug the RCA end into an input (RCA spot) on the receiver. Run speaker wire from either the left or right side of the receiver to a center channel speaker.

I have an old-school 100 watt x 2 receiver with a five band EQ and a loudness switch. Since my receiver only plays sound out of the left side (the receiver is slowly dying) I hooked up a center channel speaker to it.

To save space on my desk I put my computer monitor on top of my center channel speaker. I have found that this was a much more affordable way to go. It also looks much cleaner than running wires to setup speakers everywhere. Now I have clean, clear sound when using my computer for watching videos, tv shows and movies over the internet.

Chapter 7: Sound bar

It used to be that one of the selling points to the TV purchase you made was better sound quality coming out of your TV. Times sure have changed. TV's used to have ok sound when I was a kid, or perhaps my perception has changed, since Dolby Laboratories came along to make things much better.

Back when I got my first big screen TV, one of the selling points was its sound. You see, instead of it just being a stereo TV it had a built in center and connections in the back for rear speakers. In truth, I never connected rear speakers to the TV since the surround sound in the TV was really weak (15 watts). Having paid $2,500 for the TV they should have had more power, in my opinion.

Now we have really thin (wall mountable) TV's and the sound is downright dreadful. Where does the sound come out of these TV's anyway? I have a 42" LCD 1080p TV and I cannot even figure out where my speakers are located.

Hence, the creation of the sound bar. Sound bars take up very little space. They steer the left and right sounds, center sound and also incorporate surround sound, too, in the same cabinet. Just add a sub and you're ready to go. This is technology at its finest.

If you are not a home theatre nut like me, and just want clear sound or have no room or the money to buy a receiver and the speakers, then sound bars are the way to go.

Sound bars come in two varieties: with and without a powered subwoofer. If no sub is included you should be able to plug one in to the sound bar later. Most sound bars require a HDMI connection to attach this to a television. Some sound bars allow for other types of connections so you do not have to have a high definition television to use this.

If you choose to connect a sound bar to a receiver, you will be able to adjust balance, tone and volume with the receiver. If you plan to do this take a good look first at the connection types available on both the receiver and the sound bar to make sure it is compatible.

Another use for a sound bar:

Another good use for this is to connect it to a basic receiver for another room. Take an audio out cable (2.5 MM or 3.5 MM depending on your computer) and plug one end into your computer's sound card. Plug the other end into your receiver. For this to work one of the cables needs to be an RCA cable. No splicing is needed since such a cable already exists. Plug the RCA end into an input (RCA spot) on the receiver. Run speaker wire from either the left or right side of the receiver to a sound bar.

To save space on your desk put your computer monitor on top of the sound bar. This is a much more affordable way to go. It also looks much cleaner than running wires to setup speakers everywhere. This will provide clean, clear sound when using your computer for watching videos, tv shows and movies over the internet.

Chapter 8: Satellite speakers

Just the other day I hooked up an old 5.1 channel receiver in my kid's room (100 watts x 5). I used a nice satellite center and instead of using satellites for left and right, I used some old beat up 6.5" 2-way speakers. These 6.5's actually have electrical tape holding together the torn and crumbling woofers. Needless to say they suck when playing music with any real volume! In a movie with a good amount of action and dialogue they sounded amazing. I used the *Scooby Doo: Camp Scare* movie for my test.

All three speakers were loud and clear and there was a good amount of mid bass too! I did not even bother to connect the rear speakers or a sub since it is a bedroom setup. The wire I used was an 18 gauge for my center and a 30 gauge for the mains.

I am exaggerating some since a 30 (to the best of my knowledge) doesn't exist! I chose the 6.5's over satellites, since I had no sub to connect nor did I have the room to put a sub anywhere, and I wanted at least some bass in there.

Later, I connected the rear satellites and changed out the mains for matching satellites up front for a much cleaner look. I did lose some bass, but it sounds really loud and clear. I never thought much of satellites until this experiment. I am glad I had the opportunity to try this configuration and for a bedroom, I would recommend this. I also think it would be a good gaming setup, too!

Chapter 9: EQ's (Equalizers & Graphic Equalizers)

Equalizers adjust the sound you hear with sliders that move up and down. Each slider helps to fine-tune the sound even further than "bass" and "treble" controls found on your receiver. When adjusting your EQ, always start the sliders in the middle position. The middle setting is what it sounds like before you boost (turn it up) or cut (turn it down) the way it was originally recorded.

Each slider adjusts frequency responses.

- 16 Hz to 60 Hz is really deep bass

- 60 Hz to 250 Hz is bass

- 250 Hz to 2 kHz is midrange. Examples include guitar, drums, piano, saxophone and vocal

- 2kHz to 4 kHz is higher pitched midrange sounds. Examples include guitar, piano, vocals and cymbals

- 4kHz to 6 kHz is treble which makes it sound clearer

- 6 kHz to 16 kHz is enhanced treble. Too much will make it sound over-exaggerated and may damage your speakers at high volume

Equalizer *vs.* Graphic Equalizer:

The only difference is a graphic equalizer has a digital multiple color light display that changes as sound is played. This can be really cool and fun to look at. However, a graphic equalizer costs more than a regular equalizer does.

Some graphic equalizers allow for you to turn off the light display. This is important because when you are listening to music it's ok to have on, however with movies this could be distracting. If you choose to get a graphic equalizer and you are unable to turn off the light display then you will want to place the graphic equalizer out of the line of site with the television or projector you are using.

Most receivers and preamps, both today and in the past (if higher end) have a bass boost or loudness switch to enhance the deeper bass tones. They also include separate bass and treble settings. Back in the day, they had a tape loop feature that simply required two RCA sets of cables to send sound out of the receiver and into the EQ. In some ways, this being one of them, I miss the old days!

Recently I tried adding an EQ to my 7.1 channel receiver. Here is what I discovered....

1) No tape connectors for "out"

2) No tape connectors for "in"

3) Even if your receiver has a monitor out spot to use (which mine does) there is no point. This is because you're taking a digital sound and downgrading it to tape quality (analog sound). Then you can customize the sound with the EQ, but in the end you gain very little improvement in sound. 3.0 and above surround sound formats cannot be used with an EQ, since the EQ will only adjust the left and right speakers.

Perhaps for music it may be worth the experiment. No digital connected devices can be used because only RCA connections are available on an EQ.

Fifteen years ago I had a crappy sounding new, name brand, 100-watt x 2 receiver. I was wrong in assuming that there would never be a reason for a surround sound receiver. I saved a lot of money at the time and sacrificed sound clarity and missed out on Dolby Pro Logic which was leaps and bounds better than anything at the time.

This was the original Dolby surround sound (4.0). Before this, it was stereo (2.0) meaning left and right audio. I ran a pair of 8" 3-way bookshelf speakers at the time. I bought a new 14 band graphic EQ (7 to the left and 7 to the right) and connected it to my receiver and suddenly everything sounded awesome! That is until, one day the EQ was on but not doing anything. I played around with the connections and EQ sliders when it happened.... suddenly it decided to start working again and sadly the volume was up pretty high and all of the EQ sliders were all the way up. This resulted in a blown speaker.

Let this be a lesson to you...

1) Never connect or disconnect any wires to an electronic device that is plugged in and powered on.
2) Be mindful of just how loud the volume is set at.

3) Be especially careful since newer receivers still have a knob like the old ones, but no longer have any indicator beside the knob to tell you where the volume is at. To check it while it's on, press the volume button to see the volume number on the front of the receiver. Always check this before playing with the EQ!

Those EQ sliders each make a tremendous difference in what you can hear. When turned all the way up they can be very dangerous.

Chapter 10: Speaker wire gauges

As mentioned earlier, having a powerful receiver is necessary for good sound. Also, previously mentioned was the importance of having quality speakers. This next section is where most people tend to skimp on in order to save a few bucks....speaker wire. Unless you have wireless speakers you need a wire to connect the receiver and speaker together, or there will be no sound! Cheap wire lessens the sound quality that you hear, no matter how good the receiver and speakers are.

So don't skimp on the wire.

Speaker wire comes in different gauges numbers. Different gauges can alter your sound, especially in long distances of 20 feet or more. Here are the gauges: 22, 20, 18, 16, 14, 12, and 10. The lower the number the thicker the wire and the better the sound will be. So then, a "10" would be truly awe-inspiring where as a "22" would look and sound like crap! Most people use a 16 or 18 gauge wire.

Chapter 11: Speaker Specifications: What you need to know before you buy.

Frequency Response:

This and wattage are the most important specifications. Frequency response is the range of sound the speaker can reproduce. The human ear is capable of hearing from 20 hz to 20,000 hz (20 khz). The lower the first number (hz) the deeper the bass.

The second number (khz) is the treble side. Treble is for higher sounds (crashing of a cymbal, opera singer hitting a high note, breaking of glass, etc).

All thru this book I will mention speakers as: 8", 5.25", 12", etc. So what does that mean, you may ask? This number refers to the size of the speaker itself (not the cabinet it is housed in). To determine the size of the speaker all you will need to do is measure from the left side to the right side (or from top to bottom).

Typical specs by size of the woofer:

12": Goes down to 35hz (sometimes 30hz). This equates to lots of bass.

8": Goes down to 80hz (sometimes 65hz). This is for good midrange. If it only goes down to 80hz its ok, but not exceptional.

5.25" and 6.5": Goes down to possibly as low as 43hz (rare). Most likely it will be around 80hz.

Ohms:

The higher the ohms the less efficient the speaker is. Higher ohms require more power to drive the speakers. Try to match the speaker ohms to the receiver's ohms. Once I had a 6 ohm receiver (100 watts x 7.1 channels) and it made my 12" speakers have zero bass no matter what I did because my speakers ran at 8 ohms. I've heard 4" speakers with more bass! The receiver before it was 85 watts x 5.1 channels at 8 ohms with the same speakers and they were plenty bassy.

Later, I changed to another 6 ohm receiver that was more powerful with the same speakers and wire and it had lots of bass too. It is my current receiver (6 ohms 135 watts x 7.1 channels). So, if you can't find an 8 ohm receiver to drive big 8 ohm speakers, then get as many watts per channel that you can from the receiver.

Car audio runs on 4 ohms and 6 ohms. This is why car audio plays so loud. Sometimes car audio will be set to run in lesser ohms, however it is not the norm.

Home audio runs on 6 ohm and 8 ohm and is therefore less efficient and requires more power to drive the speakers.

Decibels (DB's):

The higher the number the better (i.e.: the louder the speakers will play). 88DB is pretty standard. Anything lower in number will not appear that loud. Anything above this number will be louder.

Circuit Protection:

If there is too much power being sent to the receiver then this circuit will trip (like a house circuit breaker does) in order to save the speakers from damage. If this happens, turn down the volume some and press the reset button on the back of the speaker(s). This will turn back on the circuit so you can continue using the speaker(s).

Wattage:

Do not be fooled. Most manufacturers only list wattage as "power" or "wattage". This number they list is really referred to as "peak power."

Peak power:

This is the maximum power that the speaker can handle for a brief second or so before it will blow. If the speaker has built in circuit protection it will cut off the power to the speaker to save it.

RMS:

Make sure you look for this, and if it is not posted divide the number by two to determine this. This is what the speaker can handle all day long. Example: 100 watts is really 100 watts peak power and 50 watts RMS.

Minimum:

Only high-end speakers offer this. This is the minimum amount of power needed to power the speakers without damaging them.

Bass Port:

Located either in the front or back of the speaker cabinet that the speaker is housed in, this keeps distortion from building up inside the cabinet. Not all speakers are ported. Some speakers even have dual (two) bass ports. Placing any speaker, especially if it is ported, up near a wall will increase the bass even more.

Bass reflex design:

This is a newer more efficient design. This type of speaker enclosure is usually ported.

Acoustic Suspension:

This is an older less efficient design. This is used to create a more accurate sound as opposed to bass reflex which appears much punchier.

***

The speakers inside the cabinet are made up of the following parts:

Woofer:

This is the biggest speaker in the cabinet. Its only purpose is for bass. Typically the larger it is the bassier it will be, but not always.

Examples include 4", 5.25", 6.5", 8", 10" 12", 15" 18" and 21". Keep in mind really big woofers (12" and up take longer to push the sound, but when they do, you feel it!). Most people do not need to go bigger than 10's or 12's thanks to subs.

Tweeter:

This is the tiniest speaker in the cabinet. They usually

come in .50",.75", 1", 1.25," 1.50," and 2.50" sizes. This is where you hear the treble. Without this speaker everything is muddy and unclear and sounds really bad.

Paper cone tweeters are a cheaper design and tend to get too hot when the volume is cranked up high. When this happens for long periods of time you may need to get a new tweeter.

Liquid cooled tweeters are much better since they are designed not to overheat.

Some speakers use a horn tweeter instead. Typically horn tweeters are used for outdoor venues such as live concerts. This is because they are designed to play super loud and focus the sound in a specific direction.

Mid-Range: (optional).

This speaker will bring in the middle sound that is missing from most speakers and creates a more natural sound. Two-way speakers only have the tweeter and woofer and possibly a port.

Grill (cover):

This is usually removable to show off the speakers inside the cabinet.

Speaker wire input:

Banana plug:

This is the best and can be found on higher end speakers. It provides the best connection of speaker wire to the speaker for optimal sound quality. You have to twist the wire around this connection and screw it in place.

RCA:

This is no longer used since it was very inefficient. It required lots of volume to get sound out of the speakers. The speaker wire had RCA connections on the end to attach to the RCA inputs on the speaker cabinets.

Pushpin:

This is found on less expensive speaker cabinets and is still used. You must push in the pin while feeding the wire into the input. When you release the pin it holds the wire in place.

Cabinets:

Don't forget the importance of the cabinet itself that the speakers are housed in. This does make a difference! Poorly made cabinets sound flat in range. Heavier cabinets typically have a wider range of sound, can handle more power and tend to have circuit protection. They may or may not be ported. My 8" center (its actually part of a set of old 8's. The other part was blown) weighs 18 or 19 lbs, where as my 8" rear speakers weigh only 7.5 lbs. Both are 3-way designed. No big surprise here, my center sounds richer in clarity and has more bass.

"Timbre Matching," and "Voice Matching.":

These are simply fancy ways of sounding impressive when really all they are referring to is "tone." To be clear, tone is bass, treble and everything between. This effects how it sounds to you. Some people just want "natural sound."

"Natural sound":

This means playing it flat (no customization of the sound at all other than volume).

Tone is very important with movies and music - especially movies. Let's say for example you have large speakers as mains and a good size center, but they are different brands. One may have more bass, play louder or have more treble than the other. This is why everyone always says to buy a set of matched speakers. Being a true audiophile I don't like that setup. What if the center isn't very good? What if the mains are two-way? Then this won't be to my liking.

Chapter 12: Past and current Surround Sounds

Stereo (2.0):

This only plays left and right sound. Each speaker is an independent sound.

Dolby Pro Logic (4.0):

This has left and right main speakers, center and rear speakers (left and right). The rear speakers play in mono (same sound) not stereo (separate sound).

Dolby Pro Logic II:

It takes music and movies and allows it to be played in 5.1 or 5.2 surround sound.

Dolby Pro Logic IIX:

It takes music and movie and allows it to be played in 7.1 or 7.2 surround sound. This is the surround sound I use most with movies. Experiment and decide for yourself!

Dolby Digital (5.0):

Still the standard format for movies and has been around for easily 15+ years! Left, right, center, rear speakers (in stereo as left rear and right rear) and adds a sub out for a powered subwoofer to be plugged in. If the sub is connected then it becomes 5.1 instead of 5.0.

DTS (5.1 and 6.1 and 7.1):

DTS is a competing company to Dolby (Dolby laboratories). It's like Dolby digital, except in my experience the dialog is clearer. I use this if it is not an action movie I am watching and still cannot hear what the people are saying.

Matrix:

This plays a simulated surround for stereo. It has an enhanced simulated distance between speakers for 2.0 sounds to appear larger. This used to be popular ages ago.

Dolby 6.1:

Take Dolby Digital 5.1 and add a rear center. This never got a chance to catch on. Shortly after it was introduced 7.1 was, too. 7.1 was much more popular and so everyone stopped making 6.1.

Dolby True (7.1):

Take Dolby Digital 5.1 and add a pair of side speakers (one on the left and one on the right). Supposedly you should put these alongside your couch and use them as additional surround speakers, however I disagree on their placement in the room.

Instead, try this and I think you will find it much more satisfying, put them so one is on the left side of the room and the other is on the right side of the room. The difference is where you put them on the sides of the room. I have mine halfway between the front and surround speakers to better fill the room with sound.

In action films I have heard items go from the left front and then go to the right front and finally onto the right surround. Other times I have heard sound go from the left front to the right side in a zig zag pattern. Both of these matched the image I saw on the screen.

Subwoofer legend:

.0= No sub. .1 = One sub.   2 = Two subs.

Chapter 13: My own surround sounds

Think these surround sounds are cool? Stand back and be prepared to be amazed. What created my never-ending home theatre thoughts started with me watching a movie that I truly enjoyed, but I found a flaw in it. I was watching the movie *Heat* with Al Pacino and Robert De Niro. Despite the flaw and me not agreeing with the ending, it is still one of my all time favorite films.

When I watch a movie, I don't do other things. Instead I am one with the movie and expect to be entertained. Somewhere in the action (which is in most scenes of this film) gunfire was shot and it came out of one rear speaker, or was it out of both rear speakers simultaneously? Normally this would be fine, except I was truly focused on the film and was, as a result, distracted after this scene. You see clearly in this one scene the bullet should have come from directly behind me in what I like to call the "rear center."

Sadly, no one has a rear center or the technology to make it anymore, so I guess I had to! To keep things simple take a 5.1 channel receiver or better and build it up.

I have spent the last decade dreaming of how to make home theatre better, specifically how to add a rear center. Originally my thought was to have both a 6.1 and 7.1 channel system running at the same time in the same room. However 6.1 didn't last long and I discovered that if you run audio cables out of a device (DVD player for instance) with one type of wire (analog) to one receiver and a digital connection to the other at the same time, it will work but sound wrong. What I mean by wrong is the digital one will play faster than the analog. This results in an echo from each speaker as sound passes through it. I knew I could do better than this, but I was not sure how until now.

The following surround sounds are all based on a 7.1 channel with modifications. 7.1 means it includes a left front speaker, center speaker, right front speaker, left rear speaker, right rear speaker, a pair of side speakers and a single powered subwoofer. Refer to my chapter on diagrams for assistance in explaining all of this.

8.2:

Adds a rear center and adds a second sub.

9.2:

Takes away the rear center and instead adds a second pair of main speakers. Place the 2nd pair of main speakers up much higher than the other main speakers.

10.2:

9.2 Plus a rear center.

11.2:

This adds two additional pairs of main speakers (3 pair total). Another option is to instead run two pairs of main speakers and two pairs of surrounds, and do not include a rear center.

12.2:

As much as I love speakers, even I think this one is totally unnecessary, but cool at the same time. I list this simply because it can be done. I ran it and went back to 10.2. This setup adds a rear center and either two additional pairs of main speakers (3 pair total) or adds a 2nd pair of main and a 2nd pair of rear speakers.

14.2:

Wow, really, who needs this one you may ask. I have two answers to this.

1) If you have a huge room and are concerned about not getting enough sound to fill in the gaps.

2) You hate your neighbor and wish to be evicted from your current apartment home very soon.

15.2:

14.2 plus a second rear center or substitute both rear centers for another pair of matching speakers. This is for anyone wanting 14.2 but wants more surround sound. Unless you have a really long couch, I cannot think of a reason for this other than that it can be done.

In my opinion 7.2 is nice, 8.2 is a must-have minimum system to run. 10.2 is what everyone should aspire to in their main movie room. In a bedroom or den where it is not the primary surround sound system, 5.0 is nice. Even 3.0 (left right and center) or a sound bar is still very nice. Adding a sub to any of these is even better.

My 8.2, 10.2, 11.2, 12.2, 14.2 and even 15.2 channel surround sounds are different from what you will read about online. For instance Wikipedia references someone who originally designed some of them. They also mention that most people focus on what is in front of them and not behind them. This is why their versions have more speakers up front. I personally believe they are wrong!

I believe you need an equal amount of speakers up front as you do in the back. This is one of the reasons why my versions are different. Whatever version you choose is ultimately up to you.

I think a rear center is the most important speaker to add to your system. Even if you simply have a 5.1 system try adding in an amplified rear center like I did and you will be glad you did!

Chapter 14: Cables

Audio cables:

RCA:

1 red and 1 white tipped connection. Most people use the red for the right side and white for the left side. You can reverse this if you prefer, as long as you do it the same way at both ends. This cable provides tape quality (analog) sound.

Toslink (A.K.A. Digital Optical):

Single wire provided for both left and right CD (digital) quality sound.

Digital Coax:

This is a special RCA cable. This is usually orange in color and provides CD quality sound. It is a single wire for both left and right audio.

Note: Most cables and wires are sold in meters. 1 meter equals approximately 3 feet in length. Common lengths (measured in feet) are 3, 6, 12 and 25. The most commonly needed length is 6 feet.

Video cables:

Component:

720p resolution. All three ends are for video (red, blue and green). Some component cables are a five wire cable. If so, it is the same three wire, plus a white wire and second red wire which are both for audio.

Composite:

480i resolution. 3 wires (red, white, and yellow), the yellow is for video and the rest are for audio.

S-video:

Single wire. 480i resolution. This is an older format that is not used much any more.

Resolutions:

480: This is standard definition.

720: This is considered by most to be an entry level hi-definition picture quality. Others argue it's not and its only EDTV (extended definition).

1080i: This is hi-definition.

1080p: This is also hi-definition, but better than 1080i.

Audio and video (all in one cable) cables:

HDMI:

This is the best connection. It is a single wire and it provides 1080p with digital sound.

Coaxial:

Also commonly referred to as "coax", this is the worst resolution. All cable companies use this and so do all satellite companies. This is a single wire. It is used on TVs and screws in on the "antenna in" spot. It is 480 resolution.

In their defense, cable and satellite companies supply hardware to upconvert this signal into your home to make it look much better. The hardware they use is referred to as either a cable box, DVR, or receiver.

Component:

This is a five wire connection. It is the same three wire component as listed above with one difference; it also has a white and a second red wire for audio. Unlike RCA these audio cables are digital. This is 1080i.

Chapter 15: What is needed to protect your home theater:

Surge protector:

This is better than plugging directly into the wall. This will help somewhat with protecting your electronic devices against power surges and spikes.

Surge suppressor:

This is what I use. These can actually protect your investment. Most also include a warranty against damage caused while connected to this.

Line conditioner:

First off, most people will never need this device. If however, you have issues with your power levels remaining at a constant level than this is for you! It is a combination surge suppressor and back up power supply in one. The back up power is used to maintain constant levels of performance. It will not work if the power is out.

Chapter 16: How to wire it all up

So at this point, I'm sure you're anxious to get started. If you already have a 7.1 channel receiver you are at the same starting point that I was at. If you have a 5.1 channel receiver, that is ok, too. With a 5.1 channel system you build it up to everything except the side speakers.

If you do not have a 5.1 or greater receiver you will need to get one. Here is what to look for as a minimum when buying a new receiver:

100 watts x 5 or 100 watts x 7 (preferred) if measured at 8 ohms, (or 135 watts x 5 or 7 if measured at 6 ohms if you plan to use speakers 8" or larger). Ideally you want HDMI capabilities for DVD, Blu-ray and game systems. This will give you the best picture and sound. If not, component connections are ok too!

Once you have a 5.1 or 7.1 system you will notice the following connection problems:

1) How do I connect a second sub (.2)? Some receivers have this. They are 7.2 receivers and not 7.1.

2) How do I connect a rear center?

3) Where does the 2nd and/or 3rd pair of surrounds go?

4) Where do I connect the 2nd pair of main left and right speakers? This might not be a problem since your receiver may support a second pair of main speakers (some do). Even if they do, they may not allow them to be played simultaneously.

5) Where do I connect the 3rd pair of main left and right speakers?

6) If going with a 15.2 channel system where does the second rear center go?

Safety Disclaimer:

Let me start off with this small safety disclaimer. Myself (the author of this book) the company I represent (Premium Audio) and the publisher of this e-book (Voltaire Publishing) cannot be held accountable for anything that could possibly go wrong. This includes fire, any damage at all to any electrical components (receiver, speakers, etc.), any harm to you when using a knife or connecting any wires or cables. This is because I am giving you the directions, but it is up to you to determine if you want to follow them. Since you are doing the work unsupervised we cannot be held accountable. No one is forcing you to do any of this work. It is up to you. We (me, Premium Audio and Voltaire Publishing) simply provided you with how it could be done. Please proceed with the utmost caution if you decide to do any of this.

***

In addition to the 5.1 or 5.2 or 7.1 or 7.2 channel receiver you have and all of the speakers already connected to it, here is what else you will need:

1) Electrical tape

2) Wire cutters

3) Utility knife

4) RCA cables to be cut up. You will need one of these if connecting only the rear center. If also connecting one pair of additional front speakers you will need two more RCA cables to cut up. If adding in an EQ for the front center you will need two more RCA cables to cut up.

5) A rear center channel speaker.

6) One or two subs depending on how many you have and intend to use. All of my different configurations allow for up to two subs.

7) Lots more speaker wire. This is to be determined by measuring

the how far away the speakers will be from the appropriate receivers and how many speakers you are hooking up. Please measure ahead of time to have a rough estimate. Allow for not just distance in a straight line, but also for running behind furniture and perhaps going over door frames, too.

8) Lots more speakers (see diagrams).

9) Two additional receivers (one for the rear center and one for all of the additional front speakers). In order to run a 14.2 or 15.2 channel system both of these additional receivers need to be able to play two pairs of speakers simultaneously. The exception is for the front speakers. If your 5.1 or better receiver can support two pairs of main speakers simultaneously, the receiver you need for the additional front speakers only has to be able to power one pair of speakers at a time.

10) Surge suppressors. If you already are running one then you will probably only need to purchase one more. If you are running without one I strongly recommend you purchase at least two of them.

Running without a surge suppressor is very unwise. What's worse is, if instead of a surge suppressor or protector you are running a series of extension cords plugged into each other to provide all the electrical outlets. That is an electrical fire just waiting to happen! Most surge protectors and suppressors come with either six or eight electrical outlets on them. Do not use extension cords.

11) A/V cables (if you do not already have the 5.1 or better system hooked up to your TV, blu-ray, DVD, streaming device, etc.). Take a good look at your receiver and the components you plan to use to determine what cables are needed, how many, and the appropriate length needed for each wire.

12) Lots of time and patience. Do not rush. Do this safely.

13) A small board or piece of cardboard to safely do cuts on when

using your utility knife so you do not damage the surface underneath. *Myself, Premium Audio and Voltaire publishing cannot be held accountable for you damaging the surface to your floor, countertop or table that you choose to make these cuts on top of, or yourself or others nearby.*

14) A tape measure to determine how much speaker wire you will need.

15) Scissors (to cut the electrical tape).

***

Connecting additional speaker(s) to go beyond what your surround sound receiver is capable of:

To add additional speakers that your 5.1 or greater receiver has no place for will require some work on your part.

If you simply splice wire it will not work. This is because your existing receiver is only designed to handle so many speakers at a time. Splicing the wire will cause the receiver to automatically power down to protect itself. This is because it will sense the additional spliced-in speaker(s) you have added and it will not know what to do with them. Trust me on this, I know…. I tried this over a decade ago!

How to connect the additional speaker(s)

1) Cut one end off one set of RCA cables

2) Splice speaker wire at one end so one end goes to another receiver and the other end gets wired into RCA cables. The RCA cables then connect to an input of your choice on a second receiver (for example: auxiliary, tape or CD).

3) For safety, make sure you use electrical tape over all wires you are splicing, after you twist the wires together. This is because you

do not want the wrong wires to touch (referred to as cross) since electrical current is running thru them. Do not be cheap about the amount of electrical tape you use. The roll is super inexpensive (I buy mine at the dollar store for a whole roll). I go over every wire a second time just to be sure it's safe.

4) Run speaker wire from another receiver to the additional speaker(s) you want to connect.

5) Power on the receiver.

6) Select the input you have plugged the RCA cables into.

7) On your surround sound receiver you will need to boost the volume for the individual speaker(s) you have spliced into. You may not have to turn up the volume knob (master volume) on the surround sound receiver to accomplish this. If you are unsure how to do this please refer to your user manual that came with the receiver for help with these menu settings. You want to turn up the volume on the spliced into speakers because when you splice you are reducing the single strength (volume) in half on each speaker. A weak signal equals little or no sound!

8) Turn up the volume some on the other receiver since RCA cables require more power than speaker wire does.

Perhaps this description will better explain the wire splicing process:

Looking closely at a speaker wire you will see that each end has two wires running alongside each other. You will need to separate these two about an inch apart at each end. To do this, carefully use a utility knife to cut the two apart a little and then you can pull back on two pieces to further separate them.

Use a utility knife or a wire stripper to remove 3/8 of an inch of the insulation off the ends of each side of the wire. The insulation is the protective coating on the outside of the wire. This will reveal the bare wire strands.

Next, twist together the bare wire strands on each side to another wire or to a RCA cord that you have already cut the end off of.

Once you are sure they are secure, you will need to apply electrical tape over the newly twisted together wire. The tape is used for safety.

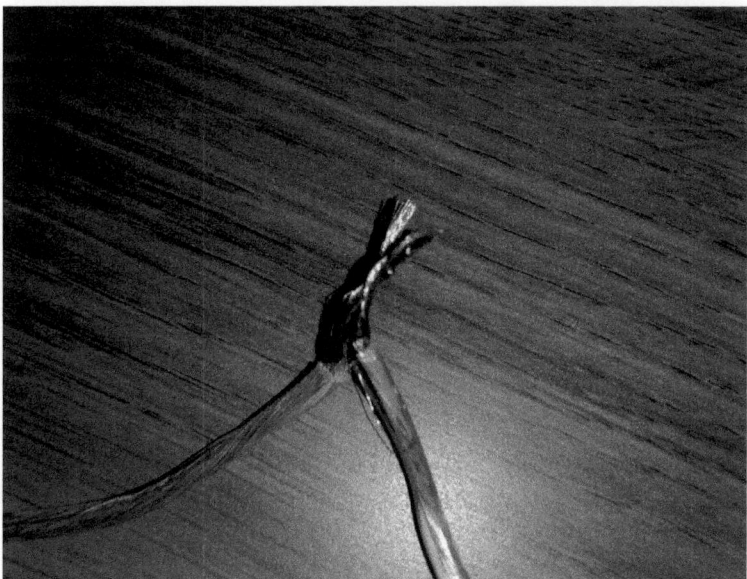

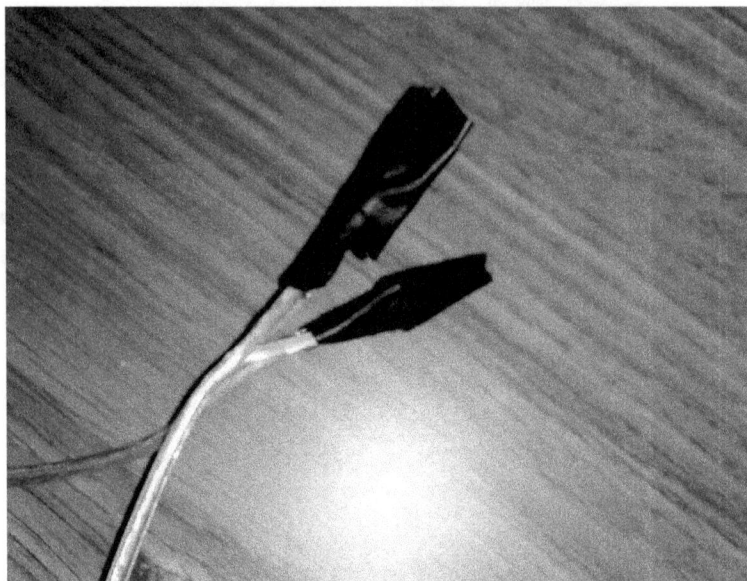

Chapter 17: Here is why it works:

Spliced speaker wire to an RCA cable, which is then plugged into the RCA input on the 2nd receiver, makes the sound become an input. The sound then plays out of the other speakers just as if you had a DVD player connected to your receiver and wanted to hear the sound out of your speakers.

For a second pair of surrounds you will not need a second separate receiver in the back if the receiver you are using for the rear center allows for more than one pair of speakers to be played simultaneously. I would advise NOT using a separate receiver for the second pair of surrounds. Only use one separate receiver in the back not two.

Instead, use one receiver for the rear center and for the second set of surrounds. This is because you will have too much splicing and therefore too little signal to send everywhere, even with amplification thru a receiver.

To connect a second pair of surrounds to the receiver that has a rear center simply attach speaker wire from the speakers to the second receiver. No splicing will be needed for this.

If you are adding surrounds to the receiver and there is not going to be a rear center please refer to "how to connect additional speaker(s)." All of the steps will be the same.

Chapter 18: How to hookup dual (two) subs

This idea started out as a theory that I felt compelled after an hour of deep thought to explore and test. My theory was that the .1 (one sub) and .2 (dual subs) are merely RCA outs with no amplification from the surround sound receiver. I tested this with my existing 7.1 channel receiver that is 135 watts x 7. Notice it is not rated as 135 watts x 7.1.

This means it is really powering 135 watts to the left, right, center, surround left and surround right, left side and right side, but not the sub. We know that they have not made passive subs in ages, so any sub you buy to connect to a setup like this will be powered by its own built in amp.

So why does it cost so much more (typically around $50 more) to buy a 7.2 channel receiver instead of the same brand and wattage as a 7.1? What is the difference? The difference is the 7.2 channel receiver has two RCA outs labeled for subwoofers instead of simply one.

But, wait, my receiver has a menu setting where I can control how powerful the sub is, or does it?

I discovered that all the menu setting actually does is decrease the amount of low level frequencies that are going to get to the main speakers. Instead, they are sent to the sub by using an RCA connector on my receiver. So really this is a built in crossover in the menu setting.

Since pretty much everyone uses smaller speakers today (satellites and bookshelf speakers) they need a powered sub to handle the real bass. Since powered subs all come with their own amp, crossover, and volume I discovered that my theory has merit.

Now for the test:

If you purchase an Y adaptor and plug it into the sub connection on the receiver it will give you two places on the connector to connect your subs. Guess what, it works!

You may want to increase the sub volume on the receiver since you have two subs now connected, but that is up to you. Each sub can be adjusted on the subs themselves for both volume and how much bass you get. The bass level is adjusted by the subs built in crossovers. Please refer to your subs manual on how to adjust this. You need not worry about if the subs are the same wattage since you can adjust them independently on the subs themselves.

Chapter 19: Additional speaker placement

With the addition of all or some of these additional speakers, I feel that I should provide some guidance in where and how to place them. Keep in mind, no matter what I suggest, you are in ultimate control. With some trial and error you will be able to fine-tune this to make the best possible setup for your room. Room size and acoustics do matter.

If you're even more of a home theatre fanatic than me; try splicing wires and connecting each type of speaker pair to have its own receiver to adjust the volume, balance and tone with. Or another option would be wire each type of speaker pair to an EQ. I am just trying to open your eyes (and ears) to even more possibilities! I have not actually done this step with its own EQ, since I think it is too extreme, but it is possible.

My suggestions for splicing and re-amplification will allow you to adjust the sound to your liking. Best of all, you can start out with just one suggestion and then gradually add some of my others so you do not have to spend a lot of money all at once.

2nd pair of surrounds:

Place at the same height as main surrounds. These are powered by a rear receiver so volume, tone, and balance are adjustable. Place one on the left and one on the right side (next to the main surrounds).

Main surrounds:

Powered by the surround sound receiver. Put this up at ear level when sitting down. Place one on each side of the rear center and behind the seating area.

Sides:

You have to have a 7.1 or 7.2 channel receiver for it to decode and direct sound here. This is because the surround sound receiver powers them. Place one on the left and the other on right side of the room at an equal distance between the front main and main surround speakers. Put them at ear level when sitting down. Since the standard is still for most movies to be in 5.1 not a lot of sound normally comes here. However if you have a 7.1 or 7.2 system you can have it simulate sound to them. To really appreciate these speakers being connected, watch a good action movie such as *The Fast and the Furious*.

Rear center:

Place between the main surrounds at the same height as the main surrounds. This needs to be behind the seating area and at ear level when sitting down. If you are using the 15.2 surround option you will have two rear centers side by side. It is doubtful anyone will need 15.2. I present it only because it is possible. The sound for this will be adjustable from the rear receiver for both volume and tone.

2nd pair of main speakers:

You want the bottom of them three feet or more off the ground. This will increase the clarity of sound from what is being sent to your main speakers from your surround sound receiver. Because this second pair is connected you will be able to adjust your volume, balance and tone for these from the receiver they are connected to. I placed mine on opposite sides of my TV.

1st pair of main speakers (normal left and right):

These run off the surround sound receiver. I elevated mine six to eight inches off the ground. The surround sound receiver will let you adjust (depending on the receiver) tone, balance, volume, distance and size (small or large).

Front center:

Place either directly under or directly above the TV. I placed mine under my TV and have it at close to the same height as my main left and right speakers. This way, as the sound travels from left to center to right it does not seem out of place and otherwise be distracting. This speaker is powered by the surround sound receiver. The surround sound receiver lets you adjust the size (small or large), volume, and distance.

If you want to make this sound even better, attach RCA connectors at the end that would normally connect to the speaker. The RCA connectors then plug into the tape in spot on an EQ. Then run speaker wire with an RCA connector attached to it from the tape out on the EQ. The other end will connect like normal to the speaker. Now you will have to have the EQ on if you want any sound from the center speaker. The reason for doing this is so you now have an EQ to adjust the tone, just for the center speaker.

Chapter 20: High current receiver *vs.* a regular receiver:

Unless otherwise stated, your receiver is not a high current one. High current amps (found in receivers) are much cleaner sounding which results in both deeper bass and clearer highs. They also tend to cost a lot more. The wattage can be a little tricky though. Say for instance you are comparing a 50 watt per channel high current amp to a 100 watt per channel traditional (non high current amp). In this example the high current amp will sound better, but neither one will be louder than the other.

Here is another example:

Let's say you are comparing a 100 watt per channel amp to a 85 watt per channel high current amp. The answer is just like in the previous example.... they will play equally loud, however the high current amp will sound much better.

50 watts per channel *vs.* 100 watts per channel *vs.* 150 watts per channel:

Contrary to popular belief a 100 watt amp is not twice as loud as a 50 watt amp is. It is however, in theory, going to sound better as it puts less strain on the amp when you crank up the volume. In fact, it is not actually any louder than a 50 watt amp is.

150 watts is louder than a 50 watt amp. It is not, however, louder than a 100 watt amp. The reason 150 watts is louder than 50 watts is because in order to be louder than 50 watts you have to triple the volume.

How to read the wattage of the receiver:

100 watts x 5 = 100 watts center, 100 watts left, 100 watts right, and 100 watts to each of the two surround sound speakers. This would be the same as saying it is 500 watts total wattage (500 watts divided by 5 speakers equals 100 watts per channel).

100 watts x 7 = 100 watts center, 100 watts left, 100

watts right, 100 watts to each of the two surround sound speakers, and 100 watts to each of the side speakers. This would be the same as saying it is 700 watts total wattage (700 watts divided by 7 speakers equals 100 watts per channel).

Chapter 21: Pre-amp:

A pre-amp is mainly found in older high end stereo systems. It used to be that we used a pre-amp for the power to drive our left and right speakers (this was long before any surround sounds existed) and a separate component called a tuner for tuning in radio stations.

Now we have what are called receivers. Receivers are a tuner with a pre-amp included all in the same device. Pre-amps are generally much better sounding than most receivers and possibly even most high current receivers. Generally, pre-amps are designed to run one or two pairs of main speakers (left and right) allowing them to both be on at the same time or to run one pair at a time and all speakers will play the same sound out of them.

Chapter 22: 12" *vs.* 10":

How and why they use a 10" in car audio instead of a 12," is based on the same principle that could be applied to your home theatre. It all comes down to this, the larger the speaker the longer it takes to push the air to create the bass we feel and hear and the larger the speaker the more bass it should produce.

However, smaller speakers push the sound much quicker for a much better rapid response. In this example the 12" would have deeper bass when it hits. The 10" woofer would have less bass, but be much better at rapid movement bass.

When listening to rap, hip-hop and pop, if you can afford to the best option is to run the 10"s not the 12"s and run a powered subwoofer with them. If you cannot afford the powered subwoofer you will have to decide for yourself if the 10" is better than the 12" for the type of music you want to listen to.

Personally, I would think the 10" would be better as long as you put them up against a wall to help further enhance the bass tone.

Chapter 23: Sound test and what you can learn from it:

The test: 5.25" 2-way with rear bass port *vs.*
dual 12" 3-way without a bass port with a
2.5" tweeter and a 5" midrange.

In this example I found I had more bass out of the smaller pair of speakers when testing the exact same music with both speakers. To further validate this experiment I tested multiple types of music from various artists across different genres. The reason in this example for the smaller speakers having more bass was the location of the speakers. The smaller ones were sitting up high (5 feet) and their backs were right up against a wall. The larger ones were sitting directly on the floor and were more or less located like islands in the room meaning they were not up against any walls.

The larger ones initially were clear, but not overly clear. Since they sat so low they required lots of power to truly drive the tweeters and then they had a nice natural sound to them. Whereas the smaller speakers were always naturally loud and did not need to be turned up due to their location. Even when I turned up the volume almost twice as loud as normal with the dual 12's, the 12's still were not overly bassy like I had expected. Their clarity was much better than the 5.25's were once I cut the treble significantly.

This just goes to show you that we can perceive a speaker to sound a certain way based upon its sheer size and the design of the cabinet, however the sound can be altered dramatically by its location. Just like buying a house, location, is the most important factor.

Chapter 24: Running two pairs of main speakers at the same time from the same receiver or pre-amp:

Disadvantage: Neither pair of speakers really stands out from the other. This is because the receiver or pre-amp that they are attached to is splitting the sound between the two pairs of speakers. You will not be able to adjust the volume or tone control independently from one pair of speakers to the other.

Advantage: The sound is further directed around the room. The larger the room, the more empty the space and possibly the greater the need for additional speakers to fill in the emptiness. Movie theatres do this to make sure no matter where you sit you can hear the sound effects.

In conclusion: If the room you are setting up the home theatre in does not have lots of empty space then I would recommend using a 8.2 channel surround sound or an even better choice would be a 10.2 channel surround sound setup. When you get into the larger surround sound setups (beyond 10.2) they are for rooms with large gaps between speakers, or very large rooms, or simply to be able to show off your system to impress your friends.

Chapter 25: Speaker selector switch:

A switch is a box with an input and several outputs. It is extremely important to note that a switch does <u>not</u> include any sort of amplification to increase the power to what is attached to it.

When connecting a switch you could run speaker wire from a receiver or pre-amp and attach the other end into the input spot on a speaker selector switch instead of directly to a speaker. This sends the signal that normally goes from the receiver to your speakers to the switch instead. Most switches have four or more outputs on them. Each output is for another pair of speakers to attach to it. This way you choose what speakers will actually be playing the sound. To select the pair(s) of speakers to use you will need to press in the button that corresponds to the speakers plugged in. Switches usually label the outputs as either numbers (1,2,3,4) or letters (a,b,c,d).

If your receiver only allows for one pair of main speakers to be played, using a switch would allow you to hook up several pairs of speakers to listen to. Unless your receiver is designed to run more than one pair of main speakers at a time this will not work like you expect. Instead you will only get to listen to one pair of speakers at a time, but can change the pair by simply pressing a button on the switch. This is ideal for either testing multiple speakers for sound quality and being able to quickly go back and forth between them or if you want a pair of speakers in say the living room and sometimes you want to listen to music in a bedroom instead and do not have a stereo system in the bedroom.

If your stereo is capable of handling multiple pairs of speakers at a time, then you would not need a switch unless you want to connect more speakers then the receiver has outputs for. Again if you use a switch and your receiver can run two pairs of speakers and your switch controls more than two pairs of speakers, you will still only get to play up to two pairs of speakers at a time. Another reason to connect a switch would be if, for example, one pair of speaker outputs on the receiver stopped working.

A better alternative to a speaker switch:

Another option is outlined in my surround sounds that allow for two or three pairs of speakers playing the same sound. In those surround sounds I have you splice wire from the receiver so only half the sound goes directly to a speaker and the other half goes to another receiver or pre-amp. This allows you to adjust both the volume and tone separately to a pair of speakers plugged into the other receiver or pre-amp that you are using.

Chapter 26: Surround system for your computer

Since ideally this will not be your primary home theatre setup satellite speakers will do just fine for this application. You can purchase surround sound speaker packages specifically designed for a computer, but it will be rather costly and it will not be as powerful. If something dies, such as the subwoofer, you have to throw it all away and buy new again since the amp built into the subwoofer sends the sound to all of the other speakers.

In the long run purchasing an inexpensive surround sound receiver and some satellite speakers and a powered sub is the better way to go since you will have much better sound. Take an audio out cable (2.5 MM or 3.5 MM depending on your computer) and plug one end into your computer's sound card. Plug the other end into your receiver. For this to work one of the cables needs to be an RCA cable. No splicing is needed since such a cable already exists. Plug the RCA end into an input (RCA spot) on the receiver. Simply connect all of your speakers to the receiver as labeled on the receiver and it's done.

Chapter 27: Premium Audio

By now, I'm sure you want to get started but don't know where to get your speakers and accessories. Going to a store typically means high pressure salespeople who don't care about you. Instead, their only concern is getting a fat commission check. Who wants to overpay for things - especially things you may not even really want or actually need?

Why subject yourself to all of this unnecessary torture? The prices are usually out of this world there. This is because your purchase helps to pay for the cost of the physical store, advertising costs to get you there, the sales person's commission or hourly pay, the cost to keep the air and lights on and so on. Wow, what a tremendous markup!

I want you to be happy with your home theatre system and the buying process and **I know you do, too! Shopping online** at a trusted online site **is the only** logical **place to go**. *Shop at:* **Premium Audio**

"Premium sound, never a premium price"

For all your home theatre needs.

www.premiumaudio.biz

- Premium Audio was established in 2005.
- All of our payments are handled thru Paypal.
- All shipments are through either UPS or FedEx.
- Best of all, our prices are quite reasonable since we keep our overhead low.

We carry everything you will need and more:

- Speakers - Receivers - Audio and Video cables
- Speaker wire - EQ's - Surge Suppressors - Speaker stands
- Audio and Video furniture – Projectors - Speaker stands

Diagrams

The 8.2, 9.2 and 10.2 channel surround sounds shown below, all add onto the 7.2 channel setup.

Legend:

7.2 Channel =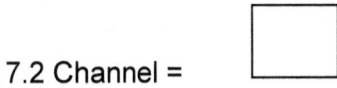

8.2 Channel =

9.2 Channel =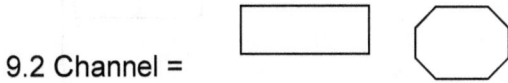

10.2 Channel = Everything pictured in this diagram.

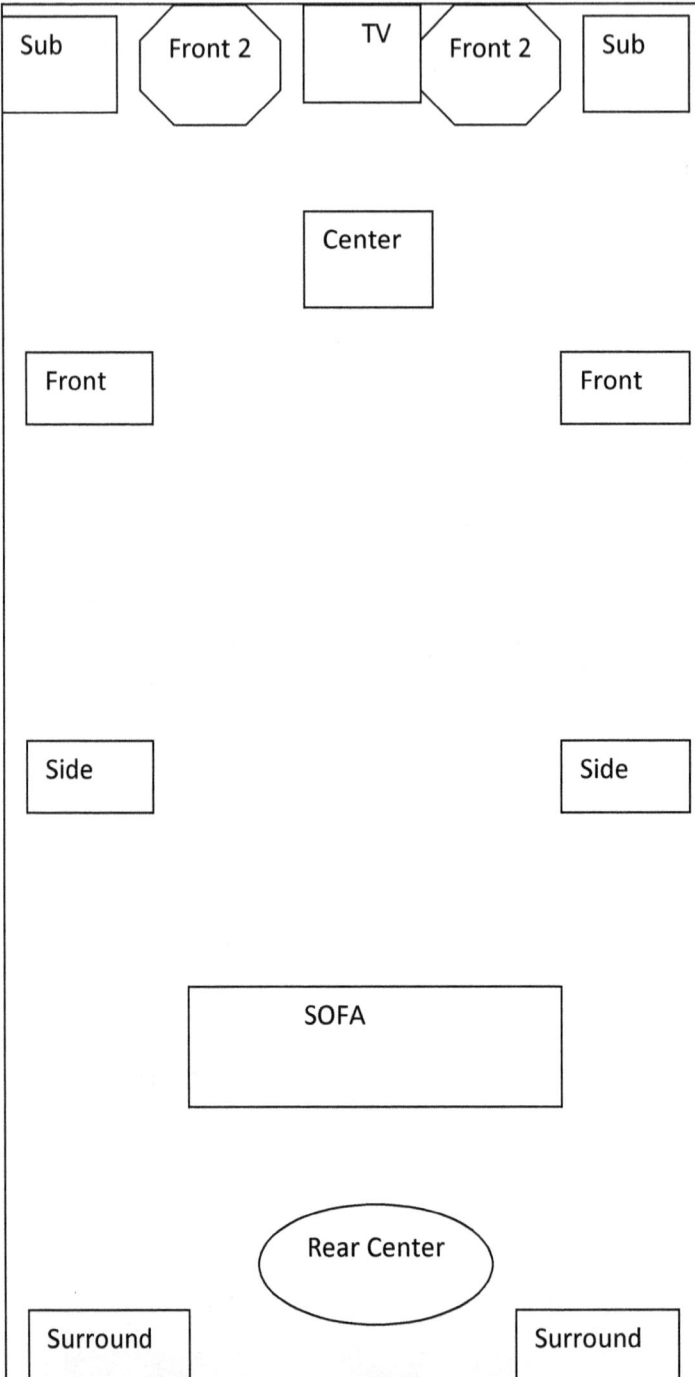

Sub	Front 2	TV	Front 2	Sub

Center

Front   Front

Side   Side

SOFA

Rear Center

Surround   Surround

11.2 Channel:

This adds onto the 7.2 channel setup.

Use any two of the three pairs of speakers shown in the triangle shape.   The choice is yours.

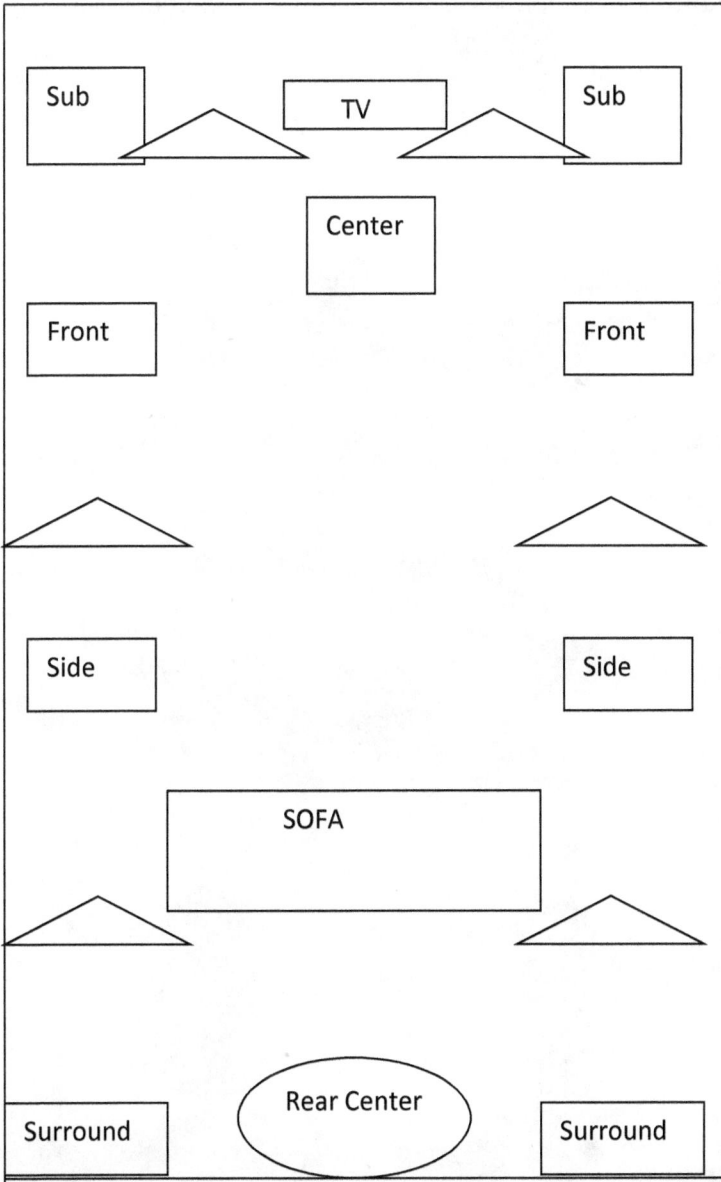

| Sub | | TV | | Sub |

Center

| Front | | | | Front |

| Side | | | | Side |

SOFA

Rear Center

| Surround | | | | Surround |

12.2 Channel: Adds a rear center to the 11.2 setup. The rear center is shown as

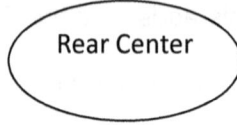

Rear Center

14.2 Channel: Is everything shown in the 11.2 channel diagram.

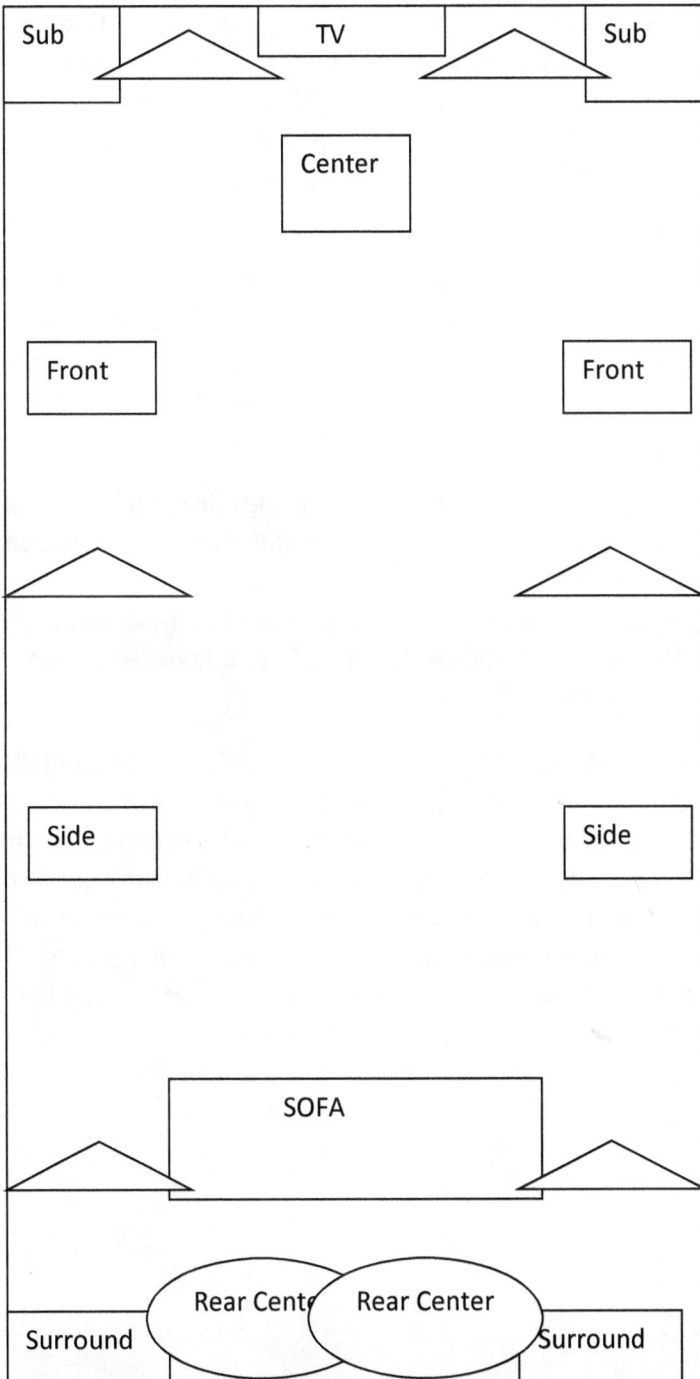

15.2 Channel:

Sub		TV		Sub

Center

Front

Front

Side

Side

SOFA

Rear Center   Rear Center

Surround

Surround

About the author:

I have been an audiophile since I was about 18. Twenty plus years later I am still an audiophile. I dip into almost all genres of music depending upon my mood. At 18, I upgraded from an entry level shelf system to my first actual receiver with real speakers. By age 22 I had added an EQ. I have also attended my share of concerts as well.

At age 23 I put the receiver in my home gym and added additional speakers to it for outdoor use. I then bought my first surround sound receiver and put it in my living room. It was a 5.1 channel system. It was then that I started experimenting with speakers, their arrangement and a powered sub.

At age 28 I experimented with splicing wire and created a makeshift sub. I used it in my home gym at the brand new house I purchased. Later that year I designed, built and painted my own height adjustable speaker stands. I also designed, built and painted a corner stand to fit over my sub to fit a speaker on top, due to limited space.

My wife, at the time, was sick of me and my constant talk of home theatre. When looking for houses my only real requirements were a room for a home gym and a specific size and shape for a living room. The room had to be mostly enclosed with no vaulted ceilings, few windows, etc. It was not until about two years after she left me that I really got started with wiring up stuff. I guess, in a way, thank you is in order to her, for had she not left me this book never would have existed for you to read.

Quotes:

"Music is what feelings sound like."

— Unknown

"Focus. Focus on where I am going and not where I am or have been."

— Me 4/28/14

"Effort expended without a plan is a waste of time."

— Unknown

"The object of life is not to be on the side of the majority, but to escape finding oneself in the ranks of the insane."

— Marcus Aurelius

"To improve is to change; to be perfect is to change often."

— Winston Churchill